Mariann Meszaros

# Traditional Methods and the Communicative Approach in Language Teaching

With lots of
love
to Jean and
Trevor
xxxxx

The Author
‿

Mariann Meszaros

# Traditional Methods and the Communicative Approach in Language Teaching

## From Theory to Practice

VDM Verlag Dr. Müller

# Imprint

Bibliographic information by the German National Library: The German National Library lists this publication at the German National Bibliography; detailed bibliographic information is available on the Internet at
http://dnb.d-nb.de.

Any brand names and product names mentioned in this book are subject to trademark, brand or patent protection and are trademarks or registered trademarks of their respective holders. The use of brand names, product names, common names, trade names, product descriptions etc. even without a particular marking in this works is in no way to be construed to mean that such names may be regarded as unrestricted in respect of trademark and brand protection legislation and could thus be used by anyone.

Cover image: www.purestockx.com

Published 2008 Saarbrücken

Publisher:
VDM Verlag Dr. Müller Aktiengesellschaft & Co. KG , Dudweiler Landstr. 125 a,
66123 Saarbrücken, Germany,
Phone +49 681 9100-698, Fax +49 681 9100-988,
Email: info@vdm-verlag.de

Produced in Germany by:
Reha GmbH, Dudweilerstrasse 72, D-66111 Saarbrücken
Schaltungsdienst Lange o.H.G., Zehrensdorfer Str. 11, 12277 Berlin, Germany
Books on Demand GmbH, Gutenbergring 53, 22848 Norderstedt, Germany

# Impressum

Bibliografische Information der Deutschen Nationalbibliothek: Die Deutsche Nationalbibliothek verzeichnet diese Publikation in der Deutschen Nationalbibliografie; detaillierte bibliografische Daten sind im Internet über http://dnb.d-nb.de abrufbar.

Alle in diesem Buch genannten Marken und Produktnamen unterliegen warenzeichen-, marken- oder patentrechtlichem Schutz bzw. sind Warenzeichen oder eingetragene Warenzeichen der jeweiligen Inhaber. Die Wiedergabe von Marken, Produktnamen, Gebrauchsnamen, Handelsnamen, Warenbezeichnungen u.s.w. in diesem Werk berechtigt auch ohne besondere Kennzeichnung nicht zu der Annahme, dass solche Namen im Sinne der Warenzeichen- und Markenschutzgesetzgebung als frei zu betrachten wären und daher von jedermann benutzt werden dürften.

Coverbild: www.purestockx.com

Erscheinungsjahr: 2008
Erscheinungsort: Saarbrücken

Verlag: VDM Verlag Dr. Müller Aktiengesellschaft & Co. KG , Dudweiler Landstr. 125 a,
D- 66123 Saarbrücken,
Telefon +49 681 9100-698, Telefax +49 681 9100-988,
Email: info@vdm-verlag.de

Herstellung in Deutschland:
Schaltungsdienst Lange o.H.G., Zehrensdorfer Str. 11, D-12277 Berlin
Books on Demand GmbH, Gutenbergring 53, D-22848 Norderstedt
Reha GmbH, Dudweilerstrasse 72, D-66111 Saarbrücken

# ISBN: 978-3-639-06155-0

# TABLE OF CONTENTS

# 1. STATEMENT OF INTENT

The aim of this thesis is to investigate various methods and approaches in teaching English as a foreign language at two levels: (a) the basic ideas that underlie them, and (b) their practical application as it shows in the techniques used by teachers in the classroom.

There are several reasons why I became interested in this subject. One of them is my experience with English during my secondary grammar school years. I had a non-native English teacher for four years who, as far as I can remember, used a mixture of traditional methods. In addition, I also had a number of American teachers, who definitely represented the Communicative Approach. Of course, in those years I did not have any knowledge related to methodology. What I only realised was the clearly distinguishable difference between the teaching styles of my non-native and native speaker teachers.

As regards my own learning style, I liked it if my teacher explained grammar rules explicitly so that I could build up the system in my mind. With my present knowledge, I would identify this as the deductive approach. Looking back on my way of learning as a student, I could not imagine myself learning grammar inductively. It is interesting, however, that during my teaching practice I followed the inductive approach to dealing with grammar, the main reason for which was that I taught young learners aged 12.

During my years at college I was taught language teaching methodology. This study made me recollect memories of my school years, helped me be aware of the fact that there must be "principled thinking" behind a teacher's practice, and I also became interested in the question whether it is possible to teach English by using one method exclusively or it is better to follow an eclectic approach.

As outlined above, my thesis has two main parts: a theoretical and a practical one. The former, titled Background Research, includes an analysis of traditional methods and the Communicative Approach. From among the methods labelled traditional I chose the Grammar-Translation Method, the Direct Method and the Oral Approach/Situational Language Teaching, together with its American counterpart, the Audio-Lingual Method. The reason for choosing these methods is that they have been very influential and widely used in the history of English language teaching, whereas the Communicative Approach is currently considered the most up-to-date way of teaching a foreign language. As regards humanistic approaches, I will only deal with them briefly, for the sake of the completeness of the overview, because they do not involve new features in the areas of language that I will investigate. What is special in them is their attitude to students as a whole personality and their feelings. This is the affective side of teaching, on which the scope of this research does not allow me to focus.

The second part of my thesis describes the research I did by using various tools in order to collect data from teachers, students and my own observations. With this my aim was to study how the ideas that build up the methods and approaches I analysed in the first part are (or can be) put into practice.

Consequently, the structure of my thesis includes an overview and a presentation of some relevant ideas from the literature, the description of research tools and the process of data collection, followed by the systematic analysis of the data, my evaluation of the research project and some practical implications for my future teaching career.

When I decided on the subject-matter of my thesis I soon became aware of its complexity on the one hand and the limitations of the thesis on the other. I could not avoid making a compromise, as a result of which I have came to the following decision:

Since the scope of my thesis only allows me to deal with a limited number of points, after defining the goals of the chosen methods and approaches, I will focus on the aspects of grammar, vocabulary and skills development. Moreover, since I want to give an equal weight to the practical implications of the theoretical background described in the first part of my thesis, I will also examine the teacher's and the students' roles during the teaching and learning process. The reason for choosing the aspects listed above is that, in my opinion, these are the points by which the methods and approaches in question can best be identified and distinguished, and by which their "appearance" in the classroom can (or cannot) be observed. In other words, in the practical part of my thesis I will examine how the teachers whom I observed use the features in my focus in their everyday practice, and whether I was able to identify a method used exclusively or I saw a mixture of methods applied by the same teacher.

I am also interested in seeing whether teachers look behind on what they are doing, that is, whether their ways of teaching are based on principled thinking, a conscious application of these methods and approaches.

To make sure the data with which I want to support my study are reliable, the second part of the research includes my own observations, interviews made with teachers, and questionnaires administered to students. Then, based on my findings, in the Results and Discussion section I will discuss how these methods and approaches are actually used as I saw it during my observations.

Summing up the above, as a result of my study I intend to find answers to the following questions:

1. Is it possible to set up an order of succession in connection with the advantages and disadvantages of traditional methods and the Communicative Approach?

2. Is a method used consequently and exclusively or rather a mixture of methods is used during the teaching process?

3. How can methods and approaches be ranked as regards students' active participation in the learning process?

# 2. BACKGROUND RESEARCH

It can be taken as an axiom that knowing a method in itself is not sufficient for teaching to be efficient. However, in order to make our lessons as successful as possible, we should have some background knowledge about the basic trends and methods that have existed throughout the history of English language teaching (ELT). According to Bárdos (1997), we should know why teaching methods change. The reason is that there are changes in society, in the educational system and in the teaching profession; moreover, even the interest or boredom of teachers and students may lead to changes. From the point of view of learners, the washback effect of an examination may also determine what methods the teacher follows in order that students prepare sufficiently.

The aim of practising teachers with an interest in principles and of professionals dealing with methodology has always been to analyse the existing methods with their advantages and disadvantages, or create new ones by adding some new aspects to them, in order to increase the effectiveness of the learning process.

In this section I will provide an overview of the development of ELT, the most important methods and approaches, as well as their influence on language teaching in our days.

## 2.1 TRADITIONAL METHODS

### 2.1.1 THE GRAMMAR-TRANSLATION METHOD

This method has been known since the late 18$^{th}$ century. According to Richards & Rodgers (1991), by the 19$^{th}$ century a way of teaching based on the study of Latin and Greek had become the standard of studying languages at schools. In fact, this method was developed for secondary school usage for those highly educated students who were able to keep to its strict rules and demands.

Howatt points out that 'however, scholastic methods of this kind were not well-suited to the capabilities of younger school pupils and, moreover, they were self-study methods which were inappropriate for group-teaching in classrooms. The Grammar-Translation Method was an attempt to adopt these traditions to the circumstances and requirements of schools.' (1984:131)

Originally this method was expected to help students get to know the literature of the target language-speaking peoples. It was through literature and translation that students were to get closer to the grammar of the target language (L2) as well as their own mother tongue (L1). It was also believed that foreign language learning was a kind of intellectual development for students; even if they would not be able to use the target language, at least it would broaden their minds, says Larsen-Freeman (1986).

In addition to reading and translating literary texts, memorizing grammar rules and native language equivalents of the target language were also of crucial importance. (Dogget, 1986) In a more critical view '...foreign language learning meant a tedious experience of memorizing endless lists of unusuable grammar rules and vocabulary and attempting to produce perfect translations of stilted or literary prose.' (Richards & Rodgers, 1991:4)

Lányi and Medgyes claim that 'this approach is talking about the language, not the language.' (1994:131) This may lead one to think that the strict system of the method makes it impossible to use the target language effectively outside the classroom because it is a kind of isolated knowledge of L2. However, in many cases there are exceptions too - students who are not only able to produce 'classroom English' but when they go out into real life, their language competence is adequate to ask for, say, a piece of useful information. Hopefully, they are able to cope with 'real life situations' outside the classroom.

After this general overview of the basic principles underlying the method, let me analyse it according to the points specified in the Statement of Intent.

## 2.1.1.1 *APPROACH TO GRAMMAR*

Richards & Rodgers (1991) declare that one of the principal characteristics of the method is that grammar is taught deductively. Grammar rules are presented by the teacher and students have to study the rules and paradigms. These are presented, illustrated and spoken about in the mother tongue and are also learnt even by heart in the mother tongue.

During the presentation of a new grammar rule discrete elements, for instance separate sentences are given in both languages (L1 & L2). The sentence is the basic unit of the language, and teaching it is codified into rules of morphology and syntax to be explained and memorised.

In addition, McKay (1987) describes different views on what it means to 'teach' grammar. The relevant one for us now is that teaching grammar entails the formal explanation of grammar rules. While learners who receive a great deal of grammatical explanation will know quite a lot about the language, they will not necessarily be able to put this knowledge to communicative effect. Moreover, students will not be able to provide explanations of the grammatical rules of the target language. In my opinion, while the former feature (the lack of ability to communicate) is beyond doubt a deficiency justifiedly criticised, I do not think that it is always necessary for a student to be able to explain grammatical rules.

Krashen (1987) writes the following about the issue of presenting rules: 'For many scholars and teachers, deductive teaching seemed much more reasonable: why make students guess the rule? Present a clear explanation and have them practise until the rule is internalised.' (p113) This does not mean, however, that there is no good way of teaching grammar deductively.

Nevertheless, this method is also aware of the fact that grammar is best presented in some context. In many cases, this is a string of incoherent sentences for grammar rules to be illustrated. The aim is that students apply the rules by means of appropriate exercises. As regards coherent texts, they may be classical literary texts (as referred to earlier) but there may also be texts invented by the author of the course book. They are created by what the book wants to teach, including particular grammar rules. (Richards & Rodgers, 1991)

Since translation is also in focus, the text is translated into the native language sentence by sentence. Translation is furthermore emphasised with the help of controlled exercises, the so-called drills, based strictly on the new grammar. The reason why translation is important is that one of the basic aims of the method is to enable students to do a contrastive analysis of the systems of their mother tongue and that of the target language. This is further reinforced by other grammar exercises including transformation, various structure-manipulation tasks, 'composition, dictation, completion, conversion, rearrangement and boiling down tests' as well. (Lányi and Medgyes, 1994:131)

Bárdos (1997) collects some points of criticism in connection with the method, which indicate that students are best at translation into the mother tongue but much weaker in the other direction, let alone being able use the language in various communicative situations outside the classroom, despite learning large chunks of the language and its grammatical rules by heart. However, in my personal experience, there are many exceptions to this statement. I will return to this point later, in Chapter 4.

## 2.1.1.2 APPROACH TO VOCABULARY

If we go on examining the approach to vocabulary according to Richards & Rodgers' (1991) description, selection is based on the text used. Words are taught through long bilingual isolated word lists, dictation, study and memorisation. It is essential to memorise a certain number of vocabulary items.

Larsen-Freeman (1986) also suggests that vocabulary is emphasised as well as grammar. Students memorise mother language equivalents for target language vocabulary items. Moreover, they have to learn and recognise cognates by examining the spelling or sound patterns that are similar in the native and the foreign language. They have to learn by heart those cognates as well that are different in meaning in L2 from those in the mother tongue.

As has been pointed out, translation and meaning are closely connected. White demands that 'translation is the easiest way of conveying meaning. Even in simple words, however, we don't always have direct translation equivalents in the native language. ...The precise equivalent may depend, for example, on the context, or on the specific type of thing referred to. So the choice of translation may be difficult and may confuse rather than help the students.' (1982:30)

## 2.1.1.3 *APPROACH TO SKILLS*

In the Grammar-Translation Method the development of the four skills is not balanced, as some critics like Bárdos (1997) point out; consequently, students can hardly speak or understand spoken language.

Richards & Rodgers (1991) claim that oral work is reduced to a minimum, while written exercises come as an appendix to the rules. In fact, reading and writing are in focus. Special emphasis is devoted to reading-aloud exercises and learning texts by heart. Larsen-Freeman (1986) also agrees that 'Reading and writing are the primary skills that students work on.' (p12) Students are given topics, often based on the literature studied the lesson, about which they have to write compositions or prepare a précis in the target language.

Both in oral and written work, accuracy is emphasised over anything else; the teacher pays attention to grammatical mistakes and corrects students whatever type of exercise they do. If correction is needed, the teacher usually provides the correct solution and does not rely too much on self or peer correction.

As referred to above, Richards & Rodgers (1991) say that oral work is very limited. Students are not trained to use the language freely, only for 'special purposes', for instance translations or drills. Larsen-Freeman (1986) also points out that speaking and listening are neglected. For students there is no or little chance to speak about a topic or to express their thoughts 'in their own words'. Furthermore, students are hardly engaged in situational dialogues. This means that interaction with fellow students is not regarded as important. The lack of enough oral practice may easily result in bad pronunciation.

This view is supported by Brown (1987), who agrees that 'little or no attention is given to pronunciation.' (p75) One of the causes could be that the mother tongue is the used excessively and is the most frequent interaction in the lesson as well as the medium of instruction. Native language is used to explain new items and enable comparisons between L2 and L1. (Richards & Rodgers, 1984)

According to Lányi and Medgyes (1994), in the Grammar-Translation Method the order of skills is 'translating – reading – writing – speaking.' (p131)


### 2.1.1.4 *ROLES*

If we go on to categorise roles during the lesson, Doggett (1986) indicates that the teacher has total authority over the class and controls all activities. The teacher is in the centre and has a very high profile. (S)he organises frontal classroom work too.

On the contrary, students have to follow instructions in order to learn what is taught but there is no or little scope for their personal involvement. Student talking time is very low as opposed to that of the teacher, which is very high. Most interaction is between the teacher and the student, and there is no or minimal interaction between the students themselves.

Finally, it must be noted that the Grammar-Translation Method evolved as a traditionally accepted practice because, as Richards & Rodgers (1991) point out, for this method there is no theory, no literature that offers a rationale or any justification that attempts to relate it to issues in linguistics, psychology, or educational theory.

Traditional as it may be, the Grammar-Translation method is still a widely used method in language teaching. There are many generations who have studied a foreign language in this way and, I suppose, there are many teachers who apply it or some of its ideas, perhaps in modified forms, in their everyday practice.

The counter-attack against the predominance of the Grammar-Translation Method started as early as the 19th century and, according to Richards & Rodgers (1991), was founded by language teaching innovations. These were based on increased opportunities for communication, which created a demand for oral proficiency. As a response, specialists developed new approaches to reform foreign language teaching. It was the Reform Movement that served as a theoretical foundation.

## THE REFORM MOVEMENT

The movement emerged at the end of the 19th century. At that time the discipline of linguistics was revitalised and phonetics was established. Numerous innovations were introduced such as phonetic training to establish good pronunciation habits, the inductive approach to the teaching of grammar and teaching new meanings within the target language, rather than by comparisons with the mother tongue. (Richards & Rodgers, 1991)

In general, the reformers of this movement believed that the spoken language was primary, which should be reflected in an oral-based methodology. They also believed that the new findings of phonetics should be applied to teaching and language learning. Correct pronunciation was thought to be essential. Moreover, it was also emphasised that students should hear the language before seeing it in the written form. Instead of endless lists of bilingual vocabulary, words should be presented in sentences, and the sentences should be presented in meaningful contexts and should carry meaning.

Contrary to the Grammar-Translation Method's deductive grammar teaching, the Reform Movement offered an inductive approach, by which grammar rules should be taught only after students had practised them in context.

While the Grammar-Translation Method does not consider listening and speaking skills important, the Reform Movement says that they are essential. Translation, a basic component of the Grammar-Translation Method, should be avoided and L1 should be minimalised or even dropped, although teachers may use it occasionally to explain new words or check comprehension.

Parallel to the Reform Movement, as Richards & Rodgers (1991) point out, there was a growing interest in developing principles for language teaching out of naturalistic ways of language learning (as a child learns its mother tongue). This led to what came to be known as the Direct Method.

## 2.1.2 THE DIRECT METHOD

The reason why this method became popular was, as Larsen-Freeman (1986) puts it, that 'the Grammar-Translation method was not very effective in preparing students to use the target language communicatively.' (p18)

Consequently, the Direct Method's basic aim is to develop students' communicative abilities in the target language so that they can use it naturally when getting into contact with native speakers. Besides speaking, another major objective is that students should think in L2 from a very early stage. As a result, the mother tongue is out of use during the whole learning process.

According to Lányi and Medgyes (1994:142), this method of 'talking the language not about the language' is in obvious contrast with the Grammar-

Translation Method. They also state that the method has direct scientific bases such as psychology and phonetics.

Richards & Rodgers (1991) mention that the Direct Method is also known as the Natural Method, due to the basic idea that target language learning should be more like learning the mother tongue.

## 2.1.2.1 *APPROACH TO GRAMMAR*

Similarly to the suggestions made by the Reform Movement, the Direct Method teaches grammar inductively but not explicitly. In fact, during the teaching process explicit grammar rules might never be given to students. Instead, large numbers of examples help them generalise and formulate rules for themselves.

Larsen-Freeman (1986) points out that 'the syllabus is based on situations or topics, not usually on linguistic structures.' (p24) Following this idea, Frank and Rinvolucri (1987) provide a range of classroom exercises and activities within a context which stresses 'communicative' rather than 'linguistic' competence, and ability rather than knowledge. They describe their approach in terms of 'awareness', an ability to see how the system of the language works when it comes to saying what one wants to mean.

However, McKay (1987) expresses her reservations in connection with teaching grammar as a matter of providing learners with practice in common grammatical patterns without giving them explanations. She says that although learners may become fluent in the structures they have been taught, they may not be able to use them appropriately in genuine communication outside the classroom. Similarly, Lányi and Medgyes (1994) shed light on the fact that although correct grammar is emphasised, it is much less in focus than it was expected earlier.

Richards & Rodgers (1991) indicate that, instead of the explanation of different grammar rules, students must be encouraged to use the second language freely and directly in the classroom. They also emphasise that students are 'able to induce' grammar rules. No translation is allowed and classroom work is conducted exclusively in the target language. In the case of grammar this means that students may not be referred to the system of their mother tongue, let alone by a contrastive analysis conducted in L1.

## 2.1.2.2 *APPROACH TO VOCABULARY*

Lányi and Medgyes (1994) claim that the approach of the Direct Method to vocabulary is more systematic than that of the Grammar-Translation Method. It helps students get the meaning and gives them a clue on the meaning.

Larsen-Freeman (1986) shows that vocabulary is taught with the help of different objects (e.g. realia or pictures) to help learners understand the meaning. It is essential not to translate or explain but to demonstrate and mime, and if this is not possible because the meaning is abstract, the teacher should encourage students to get the meaning right through association. She also adds that practising new words in complete sentences is more useful and natural than learning endless word lists by heart.

Richards & Rodgers (1994) share this view of teaching vocabulary by using demonstration, visual aids and pantomime so that the meaning of a new vocabulary item is made clear. They also suggest that L2 contexts should be used to work out the meaning of unfamiliar words during teaching vocabulary, since illustrating a structure in an authentic text makes understanding the meaning easier for students.

A real innovation of the Direct Method is that, contrary to the Grammar-Translation Method and even the Reform Movement, it emphasises for the first time that only everyday vocabulary items and sentences should be taught.

## 2.1.2.3 *APPROACH TO SKILLS*

According to Lányi and Medgyes, in the Direct Method the 'order of skills is listening – speaking – reading – writing.' (1994:142) Since listening and speaking are emphasised, students should be able to express themselves freely. The aim of the method is to communicate as if the classroom setting were the imitation of real life situations. For this purpose, speaking skills are developed by learning how to create questions and how to answer them, as well as by making exchanges and dialogues. Students are highly involved in dialogues mostly between each other and not only with the teacher. In order to get used to real situations, they are also required to speak in the target language during the whole lesson. (Richards & Rodgers, 1991)

As Larsen-Freeman (1986) concludes, the basic principle is oral communication, that is why pronunciation practice is intensive and demands attention from the beginning, from the very first level. As regards reading and writing, these skills are also taught from the beginning but are closely related to what students have practised orally first.

The Direct Method is sometimes referred to as the Intensive/Army Method, based on the theory that learners have to develop to 'a basic minimum on maximum level' so they only need basic vocabulary items and sentences. This was very important for American and British army personnel in World War II. The method mixed team teaching with individual learning. No grammar was taught but drills, repetitions and imitations were strongly encouraged. Students had to learn simple texts and dialogues by heart. It is interesting that students were regarded as 'instant linguists'. The disadvantage of this method is the possibility to forget everything very quickly. (Bárdos, 1997)

## 2.1.2.4 *ROLES*

Now I will go on to have a look at the roles assigned by the Direct Method to teachers and students. As a starting point, let me quote Larsen-Freeman (1986), who claims that 'in the Direct Method students are asked to use the language, not to demonstrate their knowledge about the language.' (p25) This also means that students are required to self-correct if they have made a mistake - a much more useful attitude than expecting the good solution from the teacher. All in all, the place of students is more important than it was before in the Grammar-Translation Method. Due to their enhanced role as participants, students now appear to be more equal partners of the teacher.

However, the teacher's central position is not questioned and this logically follows from the principles of the Direct Method. The teacher's aim is to manage to teach students how to think in the target language so that they will be able to communicate effectively. That is why the teacher never translates but demonstrates and tries to create a real atmosphere in the classroom with the help of a syllabus based on everyday language and topics. As a result, the teacher has in fact a high profile and is required to use the language freely as is used in the target language community. From the students' point of view this results in a rather limitless flow of speech, often well beyond their current level of competence. This and the claim for a "native-like" atmosphere means that teachers are expected to be native speakers or at least demonstrate native-like competence. (Bárdos, 1997)

On the one hand it is true that the interaction goes both ways between the teacher and the students and there are many opportunities for students to talk and make dialogues with their peers too, but, on the other, the teacher acts as a director in the class to organise these activities. His or her role is furthermore emphasised by the fact that groups are supposed to consist of maximum 10 students to ensure that work is intensive enough to achieve quick success. (Bárdos, 1997)

Although this method does seem efficient if one wants to achieve good communicative competence, Bárdos (1997) also criticises it. His opinion is that teachers are overburdened and students are required to be clever and need to have a good memory, otherwise the method cannot guarantee effectiveness.

Richards & Rodgers also make a remark in connection with the effectiveness of the method. 'Sometimes a simple brief explanation in the students' native tongue would have been a more efficient route to comprehension than using the target language.' (1991:10) To my understanding, this comment expresses doubts as to whether the teacher should spend precious time miming and gesticulating meaning, after which students may still arrive at different interpretations.

Referring back to the overview above, these principles run contrary to the Grammar-Translation Method point by point. I have also concluded that the characteristics of the Reform Movement stand close to the Direct Method in general, mainly in its approach to grammar and vocabulary.

If I draw a comparison between the Grammar-Translation Method and the aims of the Direct Method, it is clear for me why the latter was a kind of revolutionary transformation in foreign language teaching. As regards the Reform Movement, it had partly started what the Direct Method later continued.

By the 1920s the Direct Method had declined in Europe. Gradually, applied linguists systematised the principles proposed earlier by the Reform Movement and laid the foundations of different ideas in foreign language teaching. Further developments led to the Oral Approach or Situational Language Teaching in Britain and audio-lingualism in the US. (Richards & Rodgers, 1991)

## 2.1.3 THE ORAL APPROACH AND SITUATIONAL LANGUAGE TEACHING

This approach was developed by British applied linguists between the 1930s and 60s. They laid a more scientific foundation than what was evidenced from the Direct Method. As a result, systematic principles and procedures were formulated and then used during the teaching process. The theoretical justification came from the behaviourist habit-learning theory as specified by Palmer, according to which there are three stages in language learning:

> ➤ Receiving the knowledge;
> ➤ Fixing it in the memory by repetition;
> ➤ Using it in actual practice until it becomes a personal skill. (1957:136)

By the 1950s the Oral Approach had become an accepted British approach in foreign language teaching. (Richards & Rodgers, 1991)

### 2.1.3.1 *APPROACH TO GRAMMAR*

The approach demands that grammar is to be taught inductively. This means that it is never taught explicitly; however, the grammatical content of a language lesson is carefully prepared in order that the material is built up systematically. Grammar teaching is strictly graded: simple forms are taught before complex ones. The meaning is to be worked out from the way the form is used in situations, and no explanation is given in the target language, let alone in L1. In other words, the approach indicates that new language should be introduced and practised situationally.

British applied linguists viewed grammar as the underlying patterns of the language, so they classified the major grammatical structures into sentence patterns (called 'substitution tables') in order to help students internalise the rules of English sentence structure. (Richards & Rodgers, 1991)

Extending structures to new situations is done by generalisations. This is how child language learning is believed to take place. The way the approach deals with grammar is similar to that of the Direct Method but is the exact opposite of the idea of Grammar-Translation Method about the place of grammar in the learning and teaching process.

### 2.1.3.2 *APPROACH TO VOCABULARY*

The approach demands that a careful vocabulary selection is necessary so that essential basic vocabulary is covered. Vocabulary is very, very limited, and strictly selected according to a list set up by British linguists. This list counts a core of 2,000 words based on what was called *A General Service List of English Words.*

According to Palmer (1957), vocabulary is one of the most important principles of foreign language learning. If students are able to memorise and use the core of 2,000 or so words, they will not have any difficulties in reading a foreign language, since this word list is based on vocabulary items most often appearing in written texts.

In my opinion, the memorisation of the core of 2,000 words is in a way similar to the memorisation of long vocabulary lists in the Grammar-Translation Method.

In this approach, grammar and vocabulary are closely related to each other since basic structures and sentence patterns of English are arranged according to the order of presentation. Then structures are taught within sentences and, consequently, vocabulary is chosen according to how well the items fit into the sentences to be taught. Structures and words are not clarified through explanations, the meaning is not made clear through translation, but both are conveyed visually. Concrete objects, pictures, realia and gestures are used to clarify the meaning or, if they are not available, meaning is demonstrated with examples. When this process has been completed, the practice phase comes. In connection with the new language there are drills, repetition, and completion activities. When it comes to the practice of new vocabulary, there are mostly choral repetitions and dialogue performances. (Richards & Rodgers, 1991)

Students should be able to put the words, almost without thought, into correct sentence patterns. The approach declares that accuracy in pronunciation is regarded as crucial. This is the same in the Direct Method as long as pronunciation practice is very intensive.

### 2.1.3.3 *APPROACH TO SKILLS*

Richards & Rodgers (1991) indicate that, based on this theory, language teaching begins with the spoken language. The material is taught orally before it is presented in the written form. As a consequence, students get used to oral practice from a very early phase of language learning so that they would be able to express their own thoughts.

The approach says that the four basic skills are to be developed through the automatic control of basic structures and patterns. This is also fundamental to reading and writing and is achieved through speech work. So as to help oral skills, the approach suggests that the target language should be the language of the classroom. Like in the Direct Method, no mother tongue is allowed. The procedures followed in the lessons are built on the expectation that students should be able to produce the language situationally and grammatically correctly. At any level, the approach aims to move from controlled to freer practice of structures and from the oral use of patterns to their automatic use in speech, reading and writing. In addition, reading and writing are only relevant after sufficient lexical and grammatical basis has been established.

### 2.1.3.4 *ROLES*

Richards & Rodgers (1991) define the teacher's role during the presentation stage. They say that (s)he should behave as a model who sets up situations and models new structures for students to repeat with the help of visual aids, for instance charts, flashcards, stick figures and pictures.

The teacher is a skilful manipulator and, at the same time, by using questions, and commands (s)he elicits correct sentences. Later, during the practice phase, (s)he is on the lookout for structural errors.

Meanwhile the students' role is to listen to, repeat and respond to questions and commands by the teacher, at a later stage they are also required to initiate responses and ask each other questions to develop their oral skills.

As far as I can judge, this approach to teaching and learning must have been considered a brand new idea, even if its roots can be found in the Reform Movement as well as in the Direct Method - in a somewhat different way, notwithstanding.

Parallel with the Oral Approach in Europe, a closely related method called Audio-lingual Method of foreign language teaching spread in the USA.

## 2.1.4 THE AUDIO-LINGUAL METHOD

Although the Audio-lingual Method was developed in the United States during World War II, it reached its 'golden age' in the 1960s, due to an increasing interest in teaching English as a foreign language. For example, thousands of foreign students heading for American universities required training before beginning their studies.

In many ways the Audio-lingual Method is similar to Situational Language Teaching and has a similar goal to that of the Direct Method, but it is very different from that of the Grammar-Translation Method (Brown, 1987). In the following I will support this statement with examples.

The Direct Method and audio-lingualism both attach great importance to the use of the target language automatically and communicatively, as well as to the importance of pronunciation and grammar drills.

When drawing a comparison between the Oral Approach and the Audio-lingual Method, we can say the main difference is that the Americans are interested in contrastive analysis, the similarities between the native language and the foreign language, as Lányi and Medgyes (1994) point out in their study.

Richards & Rodgers (1991) also verify that many problems of foreign language learning were attributed to the conflict of different grammatical and phonological patterns between L1 and L2. However, the basic goals and characteristics of both the European and the American trends are almost the same - apart from the features that I emphasised above.

Since there are more similarities than differences between the Oral Approach and audio-lingualism, in this section I will not deal with grammar, vocabulary and skills broken down to separate subtitles; instead, I will give a brief overview of the Audio-lingual Method.

Larsen-Freeman (1986) indicates that language learning is a process of habit formation. This is the reason why students are required to memorise dialogues and perform them because repetition makes the knowledge of a foreign language stronger. Grammar is essential but it is not necessary to learn rules by heart like in the Grammar-Translation Method; rules had better be clarified from models, thus making grammar teaching inductive. The process is built from the smallest units to larger, more complex ones like in the Direct Method.

Meaning conveyed by new vocabulary is not introduced in isolation but in a context, through dialogues. This feature is the same in the Direct Method and the Oral Approach. There is no specified amount of words to learn but, according to Lányi and Medgyes (1994), vocabulary items have a 'strict cyclic gradiation'. As a result, vocabulary is very limited.

Pronunciation is taught from the beginning in order that accuracy is developed. This leads to the improvement of oral skills. Richards & Rodgers (1991) point out that in the early stages of the teaching and learning process the focus is on oral skills, with gradual links to other skills. They state that accurate pronunciation and grammar result in quick and accurate responses in different speech situations.

Larsen-Freeman (1986) as well as Doggett (1986) claim that communication, the skill of how to use the target language in life-like situations, is the aim of language learning. This is the same in the Direct Method. As a consequence, learning a foreign language should be the same as the acquisition of the mother tongue.

The emphasis is on speaking and listening skills because the natural way of how children learn their own language is the same. So as to improve listening skills, language laboratories came to existence, let alone the extensive use of tape-recorders and minimal pair drills, which provided students with a native speaker-like atmosphere. (Bárdos, 1997) As contrasted with the Grammar-Translation Method, reading and writing skills only follow what has been learnt to say orally.

Lányi and Medgyes (1994) think that this method is able to produce L2 speakers in great numbers within a short time, who can understand and speak everyday language in everyday topics and are familiar with the culture of the language, not only with high culture (literature and the arts) but also with low culture (related to native speakers' everyday life).

One of the teacher's roles is to introduce this level of culture during the lesson. Larsen-Freeman (1986) says that 'language cannot be separated from culture' (p42), since culture reflects everyday language and behaviour, thus it belongs to knowing a foreign language.

The author states that the teacher should behave like a director, 'an orchestra leader', who monitors learning and controls students' language behaviour. However, this is not enough; the teacher should keep learners attentive by varying drills, tasks and choosing relevant situations. For me this echoes what I read about the Oral Approach (see p17 above).

Brown (1987) remarks that students are allowed a very little use of the native language only if it is reasonable. For me this is somewhat midway between the strict refusal of the Direct Method and the extensive use of the mother tongue in the Grammar-Translation Method.

Meanwhile, the Audio-lingual Method considers the teacher as a kind of motivator, whereas other approaches do not mention this role. Larsen-Freeman (1986) notes that when "the teacher says, 'very good,' the students answer correctly, so positive reinforcement helps the students to develop correct habits."

The students' task is to follow the teacher's model and directions as quickly and accurately as possible. (Doggett, 1986) goes on saying that the nature of the interaction is still the same as in other methods because most interaction is between the teacher and the student, although there might be student to student interaction in certain situations (e.g. in chain drills or students taking different roles in dialogues). In fact, most of the interaction is teacher to student and always teacher-guided.

In 'real life', however, students were unable to transfer their skills acquired by the Audio-lingual Method to real communication, which led to the decline of audio-lingualism. The conclusion that I would draw from this may be that knowing the elements of a foreign language does not mean the same as knowing the language as a whole effectively. Pattern practice, drilling, dialogue memorisation do not result in competence. (Richards & Rodgers, 1991)

By the 1970s, it had become obvious for many professionals in foreign language teaching that the traditional methods produced students who were hardly able to use the target language in communicative, everyday situations appropriately. As a result, a new approach was called into existence as a counterpart of all the methods used before. The name of this challenger is the Communicative Approach.

## 2.2 THE COMMUNICATIVE APPROACH

This is the most influential and widespread trend, in fact the mainstream idea, in recent language teaching methodology. It is rooted in the theory of language as a means of communication.

According to Dogget (1986), the goal of language teaching is to develop communicative competence in a speech community and in a social context but not in a separate environment requiring abstract knowledge.

As Nunan says, a student 'must develop skill in manipulating the linguistic system, to the point where he can use it spontaneously and flexibly in order to express his intended message.' (1989:13) As a result, this approach sets the gradual achievement of communicative competence as the ultimate goal of language learning, which is actually a mixture of 'intuition, knowledge, strategy and sensitivity built on experience in different social and psychological settings.' (Wright, 1994:7)

## 2.2.1 *APPROACH TO GRAMMAR*

Richards & Rodgers (1991) indicate that the primary units of the language are not merely its grammatical and structural features but categories of functional and communicative meaning as exemplified in discourse. Moreover, the learnt grammatical knowledge can only serve as a monitor of the output of the acquired system.

Consequently, the focus of language learning is gradually transferred from grammar rules and patterns towards communicative activities. Teaching grammar is restricted to those areas which 'may be necessary in order to promote quick and efficient language learning.' (Budai, 1994:42)

In such circumstances grammatical accuracy has the second place behind fluency, because the basic aim is 'to have students communicate effectively and in a manner appropriate to the context they are working in.' (Nunan, 1988:27)

Richards & Rodgers (1991) indicate that, instead of grammatical accuracy, this approach has language functions in focus. First simple forms are learnt for each function, followed by more complex ones. Since functions are more important than form, grammar is taught briefly, with the help of special grammar charts. No explanation is given, although basic structures are highlighted in various grammatical contexts.

Larsen-Freeman (1986) points out that, owing to the priority of meaning over form, a number of linguistic structures are often introduced parallel; moreover, students are also expected to learn about cohesion and coherence, those features of the language that 'bind sentences together.' (p129)

This secondary importance of grammar is further emphasised by Swan (1985), who suggests that learning grammar is not enough to be able to communicate and express ourselves. What is reflected in this statement is one of the basic ideas of the communicative approach, according to which the ability to use the language appropriately to the situation is more important than being able to produce grammatically correct sentences.

## 2.2.2 *APPROACH TO VOCABULARY*

Dogget (1986) and Larsen-Freeman (1986) point out that, similarly to grammar, vocabulary is also studied and learnt by students on the basis of language functions or situational contexts. So that meaning is conveyed properly, the roles of interlocutors are very important. It is always the language function that we use the language for in real life; *inter alia*, asking and giving information or giving, accepting and rejecting advice etc. Consequently, the selection of vocabulary is necessary in the Communicative Approach as well but not at the level of a limited core vocabulary. In order to give meaning to utterances, there should always be a communicative event (also called social context).

Swan (1985) quotes Widdowson, who states that students are not able to interpret the lexical utterance properly when they are only aware of its lexical and structural meaning. 'In order to grasp its real value in a specific situation, he [the student] must have learnt an additional rule about how the utterance can be used.' (p75) Teachers should make students familiar with not only structural rules and vocabulary items but they also have to teach them how and when these items can be used. This is the reason why communicative methodologists support the idea of using authentic materials.

Among other authors, Richards & Rodgers (1991) also emphasise the importance of using authentic materials because they offer the opportunity to develop an understanding of how the language works, since these texts are created by native speakers for native speakers for real-life communication and not for educational purposes. This idea in language teaching helps students feel themselves in lifelike situations and not in ones separated from the outside world.

In authentic texts the meaning of vocabulary items is represented and clarified in relation to the entire discourse. As Dogget (1986) points out, the approach has a consistent focus on 'negotiated meaning'.

## 2.2.3 *APPROACH TO SKILLS*

As I mentioned earlier, the basic aim of language teaching is to gain communicative competence. In order to achieve this, the four basic skills should be developed in a way that there is a balance between correct language usage and successful communication. Students work on speaking, listening, reading and writing from the beginning. This is regarded very important as language use in real life manifests itself as the 'production' of skills that the users of the language have acquired. No wonder why the Communicative Approach lays so much emphasis on the development of skills so that learners can use the language freely outside the classroom rather than only produce vocabulary items and grammatically accurate sentences in the classroom.

This idea is also supported by Littlewood's (1994) theory, who says that communicative language teaching is a skill-learning model of learning, which means that the acquisition of communicative competence is in fact skills development. This involves a cognitive as well as a behavioural aspect.

The cognitive aspect means that, besides the internalisation of grammar rules and a selection of vocabulary, the most important factors are the social conventions that govern speech. The behavioural aspect is the automation of the above so that they can be converted into fluent performance. This will occur through practice so emphasis should be laid on it.

As Larsen-Freeman (1986) indicates, language practice can be achieved through communicative activities such as games with real communicative events as well as dialogues, problem-solving exercises and role-plays. She points out that there must be an information gap between the speakers if they are involved in a dialogue, in which real questions should be asked because this is the way how purposeful communication is produced.

In order that real communication should take place, students are expected to use the language appropriately, according to the situation that they are in and the people who they are talking to. If they are able to say what they mean this way, communication is successful and the form may sometimes be of secondary importance. However, if they use wrong forms, they may fail to convey the intended 'message', which means that communication fails to be successful.

This is a basic dilemma for communicative language teaching. As a solution to the problem, on the one hand priority is given to the 'free' use of the language and errors are tolerated as natural in the learning process because successful communication is possible with an incomplete knowledge of forms but, on the other, fluency is not allowed to go to the detriment of accuracy.

Larsen-Freeman (1986) also states that productive skills (speaking and writing) are even more important than receptive (listening and reading) skills. The reason for this is that students are supposed to express themselves orally first, and the other skills are to be perfectionated only later.

## 2.2.4 ROLES

Richards & Rodgers (1991) summarise the most important roles of the two participants (the teacher and the students) in the learning and teaching process as follows: The teacher's main role is to facilitate learning and create an environment in which it can be successful by all means. The teacher should act as a facilitator and co-participant in the communication.

Students have an active role; they are the more important participants of or even play the dominant role in communication and are required to act as if they were in real life in order to express their thoughts, ideas and opinions - even if their knowledge of the target language may still be incomplete. In addition, they should manage their own learning to become successful communicators in the target language. This requirement leads to the concept of student autonomy, which means that students share responsibility with the teacher in the learning process.

Finally, I would like to mention some other significant changes as compared to traditional methods.

One of these changes is the frequent use of authentic materials, e.g. letters, articles, or the recordings of native speakers on tape or video. Many currently used textbooks often include such materials.

In the case of traditional methods, syllabuses clearly described what to teach, while methodology dealt with the way of conveying the knowledge as specified by the syllabus as well as ways of organising activities. The appearance of the Communicative Approach, however, resulted in a change in this separation. In the new model,

> "all the elements are in interaction and each may influence the other. Objectives may be modified, altered or added to during the teaching-learning process. Decisions about what goes on in the classroom will be influenced, not only by pre-specified objectives, materials and activities, but also by needs, constraints [...] and by the evaluation feedback which emerges during the course itself." (Nunan, 1988:76)

## 2.3 THE HUMANISTIC TRADITION

In this section I will give a brief overview of some of the methods that pay special attention to the emotional and psychological factors influencing the acquisition of a language, although all of them use different techniques to achieve their aims.

To begin with, let me quote the "ars poetica" of humanism in language teaching, as formulated by Moskowitz (1978):

> 'The content relates to the feelings, experiences, memories, hopes, aspirations, beliefs, values, needs, and fantasies of students. It strives to integrate the subject matter and personal growth dimensions into the curriculum... *Affective education is effective education.* [*emphasis added*, MM] It works on increasing skills in developing and maintaining good relationships, showing concern and support for others, and receiving these as well. It is a special type of interaction in itself, consisting on sharing, caring, acceptance, and sensitivity.' (p14)

As can be seen from the above, in the humanistic tradition it is always the learner and their development as a person that is in the centre of attention. This is thought to be crucial rather than the conveyance of factual knowledge to the learner. (Harmer, 1991)

The reason why I have included humanistic methods in this survey is that (a) without referring to them I could not have given a comprehensive overview of methods and approaches and (b) I want to demonstrate how certain elements used by traditional methods and the Communicative Approach are also "alive" in the humanistic environment.

One of the methods belonging to the humanistic tradition is **Community Language Learning (CLL).**

During the lessons the teacher is present as a counsellor, students usually sit in a circle and tell the teacher in their mother tongue what they want to say in

English. The teacher translates this to them and they repeat it. The students gradually acquire how to use the language properly. (Harmer, 1991)

From the point of view of my research, it would be very hard to identify this approach to any element of the traditional methods. However, there is a definite link with the Communicative Approach, since CLL also puts communication in the centre.

Another humanistic method, perhaps the best-known of all, is **Suggestopedia.** Here special emphasis is put on the importance of relaxation, music, visual images and the memorisation of target language texts alongside with their L1 translations. The method utilises the effect of these factors on the human brain because, as Harmer (1991) suggests, people believe in the theory that in this relaxed state we can obtain knowledge more easily by making use of a larger part of our mind than without using this technique.

In terms of what I focus on in my research, memorisation and bilingualism can both be traced down in the Grammar-Translation Method, whereas memorisation plays an important role in the Oral Approach as well.

In the **Silent Way**, the central aim is to create a relative autonomy of students by reducing teacher's talking time to the minimum. The teacher introduces the language to be learnt only once, then explains what the students are required to do with the help of visual aids, mimes, gestures, and other non-verbal devices. Students in this way are expected to work out themselves how the language actually works. As in other learner-centred methods, here the emphasis is also shifted from teaching to the learning process. (Nunan, 1991; Harmer, 1991)

What is related to the methods and approaches that I investigate is the use of visual aids and non-verbal elements as is done in the Direct Method and the Communicative Approach. However, the striking difference is that in all the other methods and approaches that I studied the teacher definitely 'has a voice'.

The last method I intend to deal with in this group is **Total Physical Response (TPR)**, which is especially applicable to teaching young children. Students learning according to this method acquire the language through physical action, carrying out the teacher's orders and instructions without saying anything. After that they themselves give commands very similar to that of first language acquisition. (Harmer, 1991)

From my point of view, this method is very 'direct', as long as students follow instructions as if they were learning their mother tongue. In this respect, TPR can be linked up with the Direct Method.

# 3. FROM THEORY TO PRACTICE

## 3.1 RESEARCH DESIGN

In this part of my thesis I will introduce the students I observed and partly taught. This will be followed by an account of how I intend to put the background research I carried out into practice. Then, finally, I shall report on the research tools I chose and designed.

There are two principles that underlie the research design. One of them is that it should reflect on the main issues raised in the Statement of Intent consistently. The other is that it should be based on the principle of triangulation, meaning that all the participants in the research should be involved: the students themselves who were observed, I as the writer in two capacities

 a) as an observer and

 b) as a practising trainee teacher reflecting on my own work,

whereas the third point of the triangle is the teachers whom I interviewed. The rationale behind choosing them was that for me they represent three distinct 'categories' (for detail see below).

## 3.2 CLASS PROFILES

Due to the fact that my research required varied information about the methods and approaches dominating in the classroom, I had decided to observe four different English classes or rather student groups so as to gain relevant and sufficient data for my research. Fortunately enough, I managed to find different age-groups with different backgrounds, from whom I could hope to receive useable answers in connection with my research questions. As a matter of fact,

I had observed these classes before I administered the questionnaire to them thus I had 'built up' previous expectations before getting the results.

One of the classes, and also the youngest learners that I gave the questionnaire to, is a 6th grade group. The pupils are 12 years old and specialise in English. They have five lessons a week, one on each day. When I first met them they had learnt English for three years in the above-mentioned number of lessons; moreover, all of them started learning it at the same time and in the same class. The group consists of fifteen students. They are very smart and hard-working. Luckily for me, I had the opportunity to teach them during my teaching practice for a few weeks. The group had got used to teacher trainees so they were very co-operative and helpful. They were really objective, fair and talkative, never hesitating to give their opinions on the lesson even if this did not happen to be relevant to the topic of the lesson. They were willing to speak English and were able to express themselves surprisingly well. To tell the truth, I had expected communicative centred results from the questionnaires.

The other group I observed and had the questionnaires filled in by was the 8th class (14-year-old students) in an eight-grade secondary school. The group consists of thirteen students. They have four lessons a week and have learnt English for four years. Not all of them started learning it at the same time because they came from different primary schools four years ago.

As I experienced during my observation period, most of the students were shy enough to speak and express their own thoughts; they always seemed to be hesitating when they were given oral or written tasks. They used L1 many times during the lesson although their teacher kept warning them not to. I had the impression that they felt secure in the classroom if they could use their mother tongue. However, their English knowledge seemed good enough to get on with.

The third class where I was an observer (and later a practitioner as well) is the 9th class (15-year-old students). They specialise in computer studies in a secondary grammar school. They have six English lessons per week. The group has nineteen members. Due to the fact that this is their first year in the secondary grammar school, all of them have different backgrounds. In other words, their level of English is mixed, although I did not feel that this fact hindered the teaching or the learning process. During the lessons the whole group worked quite well in spite of their teeming nature. Their teacher had to secure their attention in every minute otherwise they started chatting with each other. For all this, I can say that most of them were motivated in learning English and their attitude was pragmatic, too.

The fourth and the eldest age-group I studied and administered the questionnaires to was an 11th class in another secondary grammar school, one year before the final exam. The group consists of only five students aged 17. This is because German and not English is their first foreign language. They chose English in order to sit for the final examination in this subject as an option. Yet this does not mean that they focus less on English. They have three or four lessons a week and all of them started learning English two years ago. As I saw it, they have a prospective (goal-fixated) but basically positive attitude towards English. Despite this, it seemed to me that their English knowledge is rather shaky.

All in all, the number of respondents to the questionnaire was 52 students altogether, which I thought would serve as a solid enough basis from which I could draw valid and reliable conclusions.

## 3.3 QUESTIONNAIRES FOR STUDENTS

The questions follow the logic of the research as revealed in the background research. They are aimed at obtaining information on which method(s) and approach(es) dominate(s) in the classroom practice of the teachers whose classes were observed. In other words, whether there is one and only method followed by a teacher or there is a mixture of several methods. Accordingly, the sequence of questions, with my comments on the aims of asking them, is the following:

**STUDENTS' QUESTIONNAIRE**

**Circle or underline the most suitable answer.**

*1.  In the English lesson we use Hungarian*
a)  often.
b)  occasionally.
c)  never.

This question aims at gaining information about the role of L1 according to how it is specified in the methods and approaches under investigation.

*2.  In the English lesson*
a)  the teacher talks most of the time.
b)  we talk most of the time.
c)  we talk as much as the teacher.

This question aims at gaining information about the profiles of teachers and students as specified in the methods and approaches under investigation.

*3.  During the English lesson, dialogues mostly take place between the teacher and the students*

                       yes                      no

This question aims at gaining information about the types of interaction between the teacher and the students.

*4.  How much do you usually speak in English in the lesson?*
a)  a lot
b)  little
c)  just enough
d)  more than I would like to
e)  less than I would like to

This question aims at gaining information about the teacher's profile and that of the students.

*5.  What texts do you do in the lesson?*
a)  course book texts
b)  photocopied handouts
c)  both
d)  other

This question aims at gaining information about the balance of educational and authentic materials used in the lesson.

*6.  Do you write compositions in English, in which you can write your ideas?*
a)  often
b)  occasionally
c)  never

This question aims at gaining information about whether students have the opportunity to express their own ideas creatively.

*7.  When we learn new grammar,*
a)  it is the teacher who explains the rule.
b)  it is me or my peers who find out about the rule.
c)  we get a text, on the basis of which we formulate the rule.

This question aims at gaining information about whether the teacher follows a deductive or an inductive approach.

*8.) When we practise grammar we do the following types of exercise*

➢the exercise tells us exactly what to say or write
**e.g.:** Tom  swimming every day. (go)
*The solution is*: Tom goes swimming every day.

a)  often
b)  occasionally
c)  never

➢the exercise does not tell us what to say

**e.g.:** What did you do yesterday?
*The solution is*: (your answer depends on what you actually did yesterday)

a)  often
b)  occasionally
c)  never

This question aims at gaining information about the types of exercise dominating the practice phase. The first example refers to drills, while the second one wants to elicit from students whether they are used to doing exercises of a more communicative nature.

*9. When we learn new words*
a)  we meet them first in a text.
         often                    occasionally                        never

b)  we guess the meaning based on the text.
         often                    occasionally                        never

c)  the teacher presents them one by one with the help of example sentences.
         often                    occasionally                        never

d) the teacher presents them one by one without example sentences.
often occasionally never

e) we learn the meaning from the Hungarian equivalents.
often occasionally never

f) we guess the meaning from the text.
often occasionally never

g) we guess the meaning from the explanation in English.
often occasionally never

This rather complex question aims at gaining information about several features of teaching new vocabulary: whether new items are introduced in a context or with discrete elements, the role of L1 and that of the students in the process.

*10. When we practise the new words*
a) we pronounce them in chorus
often occasionally never

b) we pronounce them individually
often occasionally never

c) the teacher only asks us the Hungarian equivalents
often occasionally never

d) we have to explain the meaning in English
often occasionally never

e) we have to say example sentences with the new words
often occasionally never

f) Are there any exercises in which you can use the newly learnt words on your own?
often occasionally never

The aim of this question is identical with what was described in point 9 above.

THANK YOU FOR YOUR HELP ☺

In order to make sure students' attention is not divided between the content of the questions and the effort to understand them in English, I administered the questionnaire in Hungarian (see Appendix 1)

## 3.4 THE WRITER AS AN OBSERVER

When I started observing the class I was going to teach I had already decided upon the subject-matter of my thesis. Consequently, I formulated the points of observation based on my research questions and according to my expectations.

The method I used during the observations was taking field notes with the aim of being able to follow the progression of the lessons as a whole. This was even more important because the points I observed cannot be separated into incoherent elements that make up, for example, a tally sheet. This would only have been possible if the teachers I observed had followed a clearly definable method, which was not to be the case.

## 3.5 THE WRITER AS A PRACTITIONER

In the classroom I did not only act as an observer but as a practitioner as well. This means that I had the chance to put into practice some of the features of the methods and approaches that I was investigating as part of my thesis parallel with my teaching practice. Nevertheless, I had to and in fact wanted to carry out these features without breaking the continuity of the processes followed by the class before I appeared on the scene. My intention was to gain personal experience of what I had observed before.

## 3.6 INTERVIEWS WITH TEACHERS

The third point of the triangle is the teachers, the facilitators of the learning process. The rationale behind choosing them was that they represent three distinct categories. Not only do they differ in their personalities but in some way their approach to language teaching as well. This fact is reflected in the results of the questionnaires and my observations. On the other hand, my impression was that one could not observe striking differences between them; still, I am going to focus on the distinctive features wherever possible.

The three teachers observed were a beginner teacher, one with ten years of experience and one with twenty years spent in the teaching profession.

The reason why I chose a beginner teacher (she has been teaching for two years) is that, as I had supposed, she would not have fossilised ideas or prejudices about language teaching. Due to the fact that she had recently taken part in a teacher training course at a university college I thought she might have an overview of the methods and approaches in English language teaching. I had also expected her to experiment with this knowledge in order to find the most suitable attitudes for herself and her different groups.

The other teacher I chose surely has personal experience and a comprehensive view of foreign language teaching. She is an English teacher of ten years' standing, ensuring that she has had enough opportunities to work out her own attitudes and preferences. On the one hand, this ten years has fortunately been a short enough time for her to avoid getting stuck in using one single method. On the other, this period might not be too long for her to become compartmentalised.

The most experienced teacher started her career twenty years ago. She is a professional of long experience as compared with the other two, so her methodological attitudes should by now have been crystallised. Consequently, I expected her to apply one clearly definable method or approach consistently.

Similarly to the questionnaire, in the interviews the questions follow the logic and focus of the research as revealed in the background study. They aim at obtaining useful information on which method(s) and approach(es) dominate(s) in the classroom practice of these teachers and whether they use one single method or a mixture of several methods and approaches.

Based on these considerations, the teachers' questions are the following:

## TEACHERS' INTERVIEW

**1.** Do you use **L1** during the lesson?
What for?
How often?
What is the rate between TTT and STT?
Do you think you have a *high/low profile*?
Where would you put yourself on this *cline*?        _____
Do you prefer *T-S interaction or S-S* interaction?
Which type of interaction is more typical in your classes (T-S/S-S)?

**2.** What types of **LISTENING/READING TEXT** do you use? (educational/authentic)
How do you involve Ss in the presentation of the new material?
What type of written exercise do you give Ss? (*guided* e.g.: translation, transformation *OR creative writing* e.g.: composition)
What strategies/approach do you have to encourage Ss to speak?

**3.** When teaching new **GRAMMAR** do you do it inductively or deductively?
What typical *types of practise* do you use? (e.g. drills, guided exercises, freer exercises➔ interactive tasks)

**4.** When you teach new **VOCABULARY** do you use *individual items* (discrete. elements.) OR you give a context e.g. example sentences or texts?
When practising new vocabulary do you teach *pronunciation* by choral repetition or how else?
How do you *clarify the meaning* of new words? (with Hungarian equivalents, English definitions, example sentences, texts)
How do you *encourage Ss* to use the newly learnt vocabulary on their own?

**5.** What do you think **EFFECTIVENESS** means in language teaching?
How can/do you measure effectiveness?
What has popularity got to do with effectiveness? Are they the same?
Which of the two methods (inductive/deductive grammar teaching) do you think is more effective considering different learners?

# 4. RESULTS AND DISCUSSION

## 4.1 WHY USE DIFFERENT APPROACHES IN ENGLISH LANGUAGE TEACHING?

In this part of my thesis I will write about what answers I found to my research questions both from the students' questionnaire and the teachers' interviews. Since the number of respondents to the questionnaires was 52, which is rather a high number, it was somewhat difficult for me to co-ordinate all the answers given to my questions so that they reflect all the relevant details and still do not seem to be a confused mass of information. As regards the teachers' interviews, they were oral conversations in order that I could obtain all the answers, ideas and thoughts I had wanted to. Due to the fact that almost every question was of the WH-type, teachers were able to express themselves freely; moreover, I got many additional, extra answers and remarks, for which I am grateful to them.

So as to get more reliable data, I also have to include myself as the writer in two capacities: as an observer of the students and teachers, and as a practising teacher.

During the investigation period I prepared a diary in every class. As a result, all my notes and remarks were available for me for inclusion into this evaluation part of my thesis.

As has been said before, I am aware of the limitations of my research. I think that the number of students (52), from whom I got responses, was enough for me to get reliable results. On the other hand, I acknowledge that the number of teachers could have been bigger. However, even if the number of the teachers I was able to interview is low, I am content with the fact that they are representative in many respects. To find people like them was my original aim.

Turning back to the students' questionnaire again, I admit that the wording of the answers is often edgy, but this is natural. It is also possible that the validity of the answers is questionable. These answers can only be construed in their inter-relation; in other words, they have to be co-ordinated with the two other participants of the triangulation, the teachers' answers and my observation notes. This is the same when the method(s) and approach(es) cannot be identified on their own from the questionnaires. To solve this problem, in such a case I also needed to apply the principle of triangulation, so that all the participants in the research should be involved. For this purpose I was looking for a synthesis in the answers. As a result, I decided to synthesise the students' questionnaire, the teachers' interview and my own observations whenever it was appropriate. The idea behind this is that I thought it would be better to provide a comprehensive evaluation of my questions rather than deal with them separately in three different sections.

In the following I will analyse the summarised answers given to the questions one by one.

In the case of the first question (how the mother tongue is used in the lesson) I got forty-seven answers for 'occasionally', four answers for 'often', and one for 'never'. For me the message of this result is that in the population I studied the use of L1 does exist. On the other hand, the sporadic 'often' and especially the one single 'never' answer made it absolutely clear for me that students' judgements should not be relied upon a hundred per cent, for it is obviously impossible that L1 is never used when 51 students say it is. This evidence made me cautious and critical with regard to the answers to the other questions as well. Consequently, I will consider the redundant number of 'deviant' answers as error percentage and will not take them into consideration.

The implications from the above analysis with regard to the methods and approaches focussed on in the Background Research are the following. The statements given by the teachers about the use of L1 as a means of making something less difficult, clarifying homework or making sure students understand instructions in a test run contrary to the principle of the Direct Method and the Communicative Approach, which do not allow L1 at all. However, this practice may be regarded as an element taken from the Grammar-Translation and partly from the Audio-Lingual Method. It is remarkable that the beginner teacher says that she 'switches on' L1 when her students are very tired to understand a difficult grammar rule or structure only in English. Based on my observation notes I can also support her statement.

For the second question (regarding TTT and STT), I got twenty-five answers saying that students talk as much as the teacher. Twenty students say that the teacher talks most of the time and only in seven answers did I find that students talk most of the time. From this I concluded that the domination of students' speech may be regarded as a characteristic feature from the Direct Method as well as from the Communicative Approach. According to the teachers' answers, it also turns out that their aim is to find the proper rate between TTT and STT, although two of them indicate that their TTT is a little more than it should be, unfortunately because some classes are too reluctant to say anything. On the other hand, the teacher who has ten years' practice says that the rate between her TTT and STT is 25-75% in general. I also experienced this fact in her lessons, too, so in my opinion she is able to use this feature of the approach successfully.

As regards the third question (about who participates in dialogues), I was interested in whether the dialogues mostly take place between the teacher and the students during the English lesson. I got 39 'yes' answers and 13 'no' replies. From this I conclude that this feature referring to interaction is typical in traditional methods, especially in the Grammar-Translation Method, where frontal classroom work is emphasised. Even nowadays it is rather dominant. My field notes support this result as well. I observed that in all cases, when it came to dialogues, the teacher was in the centre.

Accordingly, two of the three teachers say that they prefer T-S interaction because students do not take their peers seriously enough. On the contrary, one teacher asserts that she prefers S-S interaction and hopes that she can put this into practice during her lessons as well. Unfortunately, I cannot bear out this statement and neither could her students, because the majority stated that T-S interaction dominated in the lessons. Based on my observations I also support this fact.

My fourth research question focussed on how much students usually speak in English in the lesson. Nine students circled 'a lot', six students 'little', twenty-eight thought that it is 'just enough', two said that 'it is more than I would like to' and finally I got seven 'less than I'd like to' answers. This means that most of the students feel that their opportunities are 'just enough' to speak in English. The frequency of their opportunities to speak satisfies most of them.

As a contrast, one of the teachers admitted that she has a definitely high profile, whereas the other two put themselves around the middle on a cline as to whether they have a high or a low profile.

I also conclude that all the three teachers make students speak as much as possible. They play a facilitating role so as to create an environment in which learning can be successful and students have an active role. In terms of my research focus, the above-mentioned characteristics represent the Direct Method as well as the Communicative Approach, in which the goal is to gain communicative competence.

I realise that the fifth question (about the use of texts) does not measure exactly the method or approach that is used; it only gives evidence to what texts students do in the lesson. This research question does not lead directly to a method or an approach; however, it can refer to them indirectly. Sixteen students circled that they use only course book texts and thirty-six state that they use both course book texts and photocopied handouts. For the other two options I got no answer.

Based on the teachers' answers I conclude that all of them use both types of text. Educational texts (in the course books) are as important and useful as authentic materials. The beginner teacher notes that there are some classes in which students are more motivated when she brings them e.g. recipes or song lyrics since they are happy that they can understand them. The most experienced teacher indicates a similar approach to this question, that is, she tries to rely on the students' previous knowledge and their needs. To support this, students may also bring in their own materials (e.g. cultural or other) because this way they develop their range of vocabulary as well.

This feature is emphasised in the Communicative Approach, according to which the language input the teacher uses in the lesson should be realistic, thus authentic texts should be used.

As I experienced, students regard authentic materials as a kind of challenge. The earlier they are trained to get used to them, the more certain it is that students are able to use English in real life situations, not only in the classroom.

With my sixth research question (about compositions) I wanted to focus on another feature of the Communicative Approach, namely whether students write compositions in English, in which they can express their ideas. I had expected that, if I was to get positive answers, this would mean that another principle of the Communicative Approach, the priority of productive skills over receptive skills, was observed properly. I got six answers saying that students often write compositions. Thirty-four students (the majority) say that they do this occasionally and twelve answers claim that they never write such compositions.

All the teachers suggest that giving students a creative writing task is needed to make them able to express their own thoughts. Two admit that they often give composition-like tasks to their students, mainly in higher classes and in a wide range of topics like 'What do you think of this problem? How would you solve it?' etc.) Even when I spent my observation period in the 9th class, one of the test exercises was a composition task in which students had to describe a

Hungarian or a foreign town from their own points of view. Nevertheless, the third teacher says that, although she thinks creative writing is a good idea, because of her students' limited knowledge of vocabulary she cannot really use it. Even if she gives them one, the students tend to take the writing task not seriously, therefore she has to be very strict and she has to evaluate them by giving marks.

From my point of view, when giving such exercises, the teacher has to be consequent in her evaluation. Composition-type tasks should not be left without any feedback, otherwise there is no point in doing them. Moreover, giving feedback also supports one of the basic ideas of the Communicative Approach, which says that creative writing should always be addressed to an audience – in this case, the teacher.

The points in the seventh question imply how students learn new grammar; whether this process is deductive (like in some traditional methods) or inductive (like in the Communicative Approach). According to thirty-five replies it is the teacher who explains the rule, which leads me to believe that their teacher teaches grammar deductively, which is a distinguished feature of the Grammar-Translation Method. There were two more options in the questionnaire: whether it is the student or his/her peers who find out about the rule and whether they get a text on the basis of which they formulate the rule. With these options I wanted to obtain information in the students' language about inductive grammar teaching, which is one of the major characteristics of the Communicative Approach. (Grammar is dealt with briefly, no explanation is given but only basic structures are highlighted by the teacher). Seventeen students think that this is the way how they learn new grammar. However, the questionnaire results (thirty-five votes for deductive and only seventeen for inductive) are in contrast with the teachers' and my own experience as well. The teachers I interviewed and also I myself tried to teach grammar inductively. We never did it in the other way. As I experienced it, the teachers never introduced new grammar without an example, without showing how it worked and then they always drew conclusions together with the students. They asked students to create a pattern or sometimes, with questions and answers, students gradually formulated the rules themselves. The teachers also tried to avoid using definitions much too often when clarifying the exact rule in the end.

Conforming to my view, the reason for the sharp difference in the students' questionnaire and the teachers' interview may be that students mixed or simply were not able to recall the steps of the grammar teaching process. They might only have remembered the last step when their teacher clarified the rule in order to make it clear for everybody in the class. That was why they thought that it was the teacher who explained the rule to them and it was not them who finally managed to formulate it.

I continued my grammar-related research questions with ones inquiring about practice. On the one hand, I asked the students about exercises that tell or do not tell them exactly what to say or write. To make my meaning clear, I gave them example sentences too. This part of the question is based on the principles of the Grammar-Translation Method and the Audio-lingual Method, since these traditional methods often use drill-type exercises to practise new grammar.

On the other hand, the following part of the question examines whether they do exercises which do not tell them what to say. Here I also wrote example sentences to help students imagine the situation. This question indicates the communicative-type of exercise in which there is an information gap between the speakers involved in a dialogue. The result is that, in general, both types of exercise can be found in every class where I administered the questionnaires. Twenty-five students say that they often do the traditional drill-type exercises and in two responses I found that students do them occasionally. Nobody wrote 'never'. From this I conclude that traditional types of exercise definitely exist in the English lesson.

In connection with the second part of my question, twenty-one students admit that they often do communicative types of exercise and thirty-one students claim that they do them occasionally.

As a reflection, the three teachers indicate that they use a mixture of these guided and less guided exercises because they think both types are necessary but, at the same time, they all emphasise that a lot depends on the level and the difficulty of the given material. One of the teachers suggests that drills are only limitedly useful among younger students although they like them. Older students, however, do not find drills very amusing although they find them useful. All of the teachers prefer freer exercises even in grammar practice, together with free talk, discussions and interactive tasks.

The two final questions in the students' questionnaire are very complex, and both are in connection with new vocabulary presentation and practice. I will give a general overview of the sub-points of the questions by reflecting on the results I got.

The 9th question focuses on how students learn new words, how they get to know the new vocabulary etc. I collected some characteristic features from every method and approach so as to examine a range of possibilities of vocabulary learning.

Concluded from the students' answers, the Grammar-Translation Method is not typical in vocabulary teaching. More than half of the population I examined claim that the teacher never presents the items one by one without a context, most often with example sentences. However, the other basic feature of the Grammar-Translation Method is dominant because exactly half of the students say that occasionally they learn the meaning from Hungarian equivalents. The rate is better with the characteristics of the Direct and the Audio-lingual Methods; forty students indicate that the teacher is the person who presents them new words one by one with the help of example sentences and by avoiding L1. It can be said that this may be viewed as a link between traditional methods and the Communicative Approach.

My research questions also include some principles of the Communicative Approach. One of them is whether students first meet new words in a text. Thirty-four students responded with 'yes, we often meet them'. Moreover, this number of students also admit that they occasionally guess the meaning based on the text.

To support this, the teachers also corroborate these results. They point out that giving a context, for instance example sentences or texts, is very important instead of using individual items. One of them denies clarifying the meaning of new words with their Hungarian equivalents. However, the other two admit that they occasionally do use direct translation as a last resort - only if guessing the meaning through aids, pictures, drawings, real objects, miming and explanation does not work.

On the whole, I can say that the Communicative Approach dominates the processes of teaching and learning new vocabulary in the groups I observed.

If I go on to evaluate the information in connection with practising new words, I can identify a similar communicative tendency.

Both the Direct and the Audio-lingual Methods emphasise that students should pronounce the new words in chorus and individually as well. I got thirty-five answers in which students say that they practise new vocabulary in both ways.

I was also curious to know whether the teacher only asked them for Hungarian equivalents. To my surprise, twenty-five students stated that the teacher did it occasionally and I found twenty-four answers with 'never'. I also took part in a lesson where students were given an oral test and the teacher asked them for the Hungarian equivalents of different expressions.

As regards other ways of practising new vocabulary, the majority of the students point out that occasionally they have to explain the meaning in English or say example sentences with the new words. These features are common in the Direct Method and the Oral Approach. In fact, in the Grammar-Translation Method students also have to say example sentences with the new vocabulary but with the help of translation.

The last question in the students' questionnaire (what we consider independent language usage) is somewhat problematic, because I asked students whether there were any exercises in which they could use the newly learnt words on their own. I regard this question as a principle of the Communicative Approach. Thirty-four students claim that they can often use the newly learnt words on their own, while sixteen say they can do that occasionally. This result falls in line with my own view as I also prefer these kinds of task because, in my experience, students' active vocabulary will widen this way.

In the teachers' interview I got very useful answers to these questions. They suggest that putting the new vocabulary into sentences and working on them e.g. in their homework or pronunciation practice is essential. Moreover, the beginner teacher tells me that she uses the above-mentioned techniques to practise pronunciation but she does not want students to feel frustrated and so tries to make the task amusing because, as she relates, if she only said 'Repeat this word five times!', this would be embarrassing for the student. She also says that she successfully encourages students to use the newly learnt vocabulary on their own by asking them to write a funny dialogue or a short composition. Her students find these tasks really entertaining and, at the same time, they can express themselves freely and put their ideas into the dialogues.

Every teacher acknowledges that younger students do not need special encouragement because they are happy to use their limited language competence in numerous everyday situations.

As a summary, I can conclude that when it comes to practising new vocabulary, the dominance of the Communicative Approach is obvious, which I find a good way of helping students internalise and actively use lexical items.

## 4.2 FINDING THE BALANCE BETWEEN POPULARITY AND EFFECTIVENESS

In 4.1 above, the focus of my investigation was on the reasons why various methods and approaches are used in the teaching of English. In other words, I concentrated on the most appropriate ways of applying them, which also implies that what I wanted to analyse was how far they were effective.

However, effectiveness is in itself not enough. We should not forget that students are human beings, who need an environment in which they feel safe and good. This requires that the teacher should make sure they find the learning process entertaining. Consequently, it is advisable to find a good balance between the effectiveness and the popularity of the methods and approaches that we use. In the following, I will examine this question with the help of the teachers with whom I worked during my research.

All the interviewees agree that effectiveness is the actual use of language, the ability of using a certain grammar point properly and the vocabulary learnt previously. One of them regards effectiveness as the ability to communicate without being misunderstood on the one hand, and as a feeling of success when using a foreign language on the other. At this point there is a striking similarity with the opinion of another interviewee, who believes that each learner has a feeling inside about how much (s)he has learnt, and this feeling always reflects some degree of 'objective' truth.

Nevertheless, we all agreed that effectiveness is very difficult to define and sometimes it is almost impossible to 'trace', although I think that a student does have a sense of progress, a sense of achievement and (s)he is the only person who is fully competent to judge the effectiveness of his/her learning a language.

One of the teachers emphasised that effectiveness is there when students are motivated, active, enthusiastic and produce good results in testing and in their performance. As regards popularity, she also states that without popularity it is impossible to be effective, but this does not mean 'cheap popularity' (low requirements, no work). According to her, popularity is enthusiasm through an emotional approach to learning.

Similarly to her, the two other teachers pointed out that there is no doubt about a strong link between popularity and effectiveness. Students like learning when they can realise what they have learnt and this is a wonderful feeling, which could be a kind of motivation.

All the teachers I interviewed underline motivation as a particularly important criterion of effective learning. They seem to support the idea that with young learners of English it is popularity that counts, while with teenagers or adults it is rather motivation that we have to aim at.

On the other hand, they all emphasise the importance of popular activities such as games, warmers, role-play and funny tasks when students believe that what they are doing is 'only' for fun, and has nothing to do with learning. At least not in the traditional sense of the word, which means that they cannot identify the 'hidden teaching points' in the activities. To be honest, this is not what we expect from them; their job is to do hard work through amusement in a stress-free environment. If the teacher is able to put both considerations into practice we can say that there is a balance between popularity and effectiveness.

# 5. REFLECTION AND CONCLUSION

Looking back on my thesis in view of practical implications for my future career, I have become conscious of the features of the methods and approaches I studied; moreover, I intend to use them in the classroom when I go into teaching. As specified in the Statement of Intent, one of my research questions was whether a method is used consequently and exclusively or a mixture of methods is used during the teaching process. According to my observations and data collection from teachers and students, only one single method was never used but rather a mixture of them.

In the first part of my thesis, I gave a focussed analysis of traditional methods and the Communicative Approach. After becoming aware of the complexity of the question and the limitations of my research I had to make a compromise, as a result of which I dealt with the aspects of grammar, vocabulary, skills development, the goals of these methods and approaches, as well as the teachers' and students' roles in the teaching and learning process. Moreover, as regards humanistic approaches, I only dealt with them briefly to make the 'completeness' of the overview perceptible.

Due to the fact that the investigation period coincided with my teaching practice, I had the opportunity to try and apply many aspects of the methods and approaches I analysed in the theoretical part of my thesis. As a result, what I observed and what I personally did will, hopefully, make my future teaching rather well-grounded.

My original aim was to establish in myself a principled way of thinking with regard to the practical application of these methods and approaches so that I would use the basic ideas that underline them effectively in the classroom. It was interesting for me to realise that several theories cannot be carried out in practice in all circumstances. For instance, none of the teachers I observed used any humanistic approaches exclusively. The reason for this could be that

Hungarian language classes in primary schools as well in secondary grammar schools are not the most 'idealistic forms' for the special attitudes required by these approaches.

In my opinion, I managed to get first-hand experience in many of the aspects I investigated but, in my future career as a teacher, in my everyday practice I will go on improving the knowledge that I gained.

Based on my experience, I do not think it would be effective to use only one single method in my teaching but I would rather 'borrow' useful features from several ones. However, I am also aware of the fact that this is not the only way of teaching a foreign language but one from among many possibilities. Nevertheless, I feel that it would suit my idea of efficiency the best.

As a result of the second part of my thesis, I described the research I did by collecting data from students and teachers, my own observations, as well as my teaching practice in order to study how the ideas of the methods and approaches I presented from the literature could be put into practice. This was followed by the systematic analysis of the data and my evaluation of the research questions.

I realise that my research might have been more generalisable if I had investigated other classes as well and if I had had the opportunity to interview more teachers on the application of different methods and approaches. However, I believe that this database was enough to support the investigation of the issues raised in the research questions with relevant and sufficient information.

I am still engaged with my question about effectiveness and popularity since I feel that this is a very complex question and much more difficult to investigate than the use of various methods. I would have got more information from the students about this if I had formulated such questions in their questionnaire so as to be able to analyse in more detail what they regard as effectiveness and popularity in learning English as a foreign language.

As regards my questions whether it is possible to set up an order of succession in connection with the advantages and disadvantages of traditional methods and the Communicative Approach, I have come to the conclusion that teachers have to find a balance between them. There are cases when some aspects of the 'old methods' are just as effective and useful as the principles of the Communicative Approach. In the future I will follow the use of their mixture, that is an eclectic approach to teaching the language.

My third research question aimed at how methods and approaches can be ranked as regards students' active participation in the learning process. In fact, in my opinion it is not possible to rank them but, as I experienced, in many cases this depends very much on the attitude of the classes or groups. During my research I met some groups in which traditional-type exercises were more popular to generate active participation, while in other classes it was obvious that they preferred the communicative-type of tasks and had active roles. The former were rather introverted groups whereas the latter were more extroverted students.

As a final reflection, I think that I learnt very much by doing the background research and the practical application of the principles investigated. I believe that the writing of my thesis will have a great influence on my future career as a teacher.

# BIBLIOGRAPHY

Bárdos, J. (1997) A nyelvtanítás története és a módszerfogalom tartalma.      Veszprém: Veszprémi Egyetemi Kiadó.

Budai, L. (ed) (1994) Readings in English Language Teaching Methodology. Budapest: Nemzeti Tankönyvkiadó.

Doggett, G. (1986) Eight Approaches to Language Teaching. ERIC      Clearinghouse      on Languages and Linguistics. Unpublished material.

Douglas   Brown,   H.   (1987)   Principles   of   Language   Learning   and   Teaching. 2nd edition. New Jersey: Prentice Hall, INC.

Frank, A. & M. Rinvolucri (1991) Grammar in Action Again. New York: Prentice Hall International.

Harmer J. (1991) The Practice of English Language Teaching. New edition.   Harlow: Longman.

Howatt, A. (1984) A History of English Language Teaching. Oxford: Oxford    University Press.

Krashen, S.D. (1987) Principles and Practice in Second Language  Acquisition. Hertfordshire: Prentice Hall International.

Larsen-Freeman, D. (1986) Techniques and Principles in Language Teaching.   Oxford: Oxford University Press.

Lányi, I. & P. Medgyes (1994) English Language Teaching. Budapest: Nemzeti Tankönyvkiadó.

Littlewood, W. (1994) Communicative Language Teaching. Cambridge:   Cambridge University Press.

McKay, S. (1987) Teaching Grammar. New York: Prentice Hall International.

Moskowitz, G. (1978) Caring and Sharing in the Foreign Language Class.      Boston, Mass.: Newbury House/Heinle & Heinle.

Nunan, D. (1988) The Learner-Centred Curriculum. Cambridge: Press Syndicate of the University of Cambridge.

Nunan, D. (1989) Designing Tasks for the Communicative Classroom. Cambridge: Cambridge University Press.

Richards, J.C. & T.S. Rodgers (eds) (1991) Approaches and Methods in   Language Teaching. A Description and Analysis. Cambridge:   Cambridge University Press.

Swan, M. (1985) A Critical Look at the Communicative Approach. ELT Journal   39/1 and 39/2

Wright, T. (1994) Investigating English. London: Edward Arnold.